Jumpers At the Gate of Hell

(More than a book)

Anthony Ebubechwuku Orji

Jumpers At the Gate of Hell:

ISBN: 978-978-950-953-9
Publishers:
 Write-for-Me,
No. 2 St. Finbarrs College Road, by Bright Oridami Street,
Akoka, Yaba, Lagos, Nigeria.
www.writeforme.com.ng
Tel.: +234 803 4748 093, +234 818 399 7678

Contents

Dedication

I dedicate this book to the Almighty God who has called me out of darkness into His marvelous light.

Acknowledgement

My profound gratitude goes to my family: Mrs Aghatha Imoh, Mrs.Joy Orji, Adaeze, Chinaza, Ezekiel, Chigaemezu, Francis and Victor. I owe my down to earth gratitude to my mother who works in the Nigerian Defence Acedemy, she taught me just as the mother eagle teaches her eaglets how to fly, these past years. I remember my able lecturer at the Academy, Dr. Vym Dan.

Finally I wish to acknowledge the editor of this book, Brother Oladayo James, who through the divine wisdom of God edited this book excellently.

I pray that God almighty will bless all of you. Amen

Forward

Jumpers at the Gate of Hell is more than a book; it is an insightful revelation concerning the patriarchs of old (The faith of our Fathers) and the two ends of eternity. Brother Paul in his conversations with ancient elders has been inspired by God to write these things for our edification. Just as there is both doctrinal and chronological approach to the Holy bible, so also this inspirational book follows both doctrinal and chronological order. It is both timely and accurate for our generation and full of scriptures. Read it and increase in knowledge, obey it and be wise, retain it and be established.

Introduction

"And these all, having obtained a good report through faith, received not the promise: God having provided some better thing for us, that they without us should not be made perfect.

Wherefore seeing we also are compassed about with so great a cloud of witnesses, let us lay aside every weight, and the sin which doth so easily beset us, and let us run with patience the race that is set before us, Looking unto Jesus the author and finisher of our faith; who for the joy that was set before him endured the cross, despising the shame, and is set down at the right hand of the throne of God."

Heb 11:39-40; 12:1-2

Chapter One: Journey to Eternal Doom

As I walked across the tunnel of hell, I saw a lady who was arrayed in purple and scarlet color and decked with gold, precious stones and pearls, having a golden cup in her hand full of abominations and filthiness of her fornication. Upon her fore-head was a name written; **MYSTERY BABYLON THE GREAT, THE MOTHER OF HARLOTS AND ABOMINATIONS OF THE EARTH**. I moved closer and closer, but she kept drawing backwards. At a stage, she halted and pointed at me **(a sinner)** to come closer and drink from her cup of abomination which I acknowledged and moved closer. Haven moved closer, she pointed to the tunnel of hell. To as many who were willing to drink from her cup of abomination will be given a pearl which if they use, they will live for a thousand years. At that I took a step backwards and looked at her the second time but now she was gazing at me eyeballs to eyeballs. While she was looking at me, I felt a little uneasy and I decided to take to my heels. No sooner had I left, then the king of the **pit** came out looking so terrifying and disgusting, panting and growling, the beast who was once the son of the morning.

"How art thou fallen from heaven, O Lucifer, son of the morning! how art thou cut down to the ground, which didst weaken the nations!" Isaiah 14:12.

"Where is the fool who was here in this tunnel?" But the lady told him that I had run away. Angry and disgusted at her statement, he decided to take the cup of abominations from her hand. Looking at the cup of abomination, he drank all that was inside the cup and threw away the cup. From the distance I was to the tunnel, I heard the sound of the cup that dropped on the ground. I decided to wait for a while before continuing with the race. As I was waiting, I heard the growling of the beast. "Where are you? Where are you?" He said. I immediately laid down and started crawling. I crawled for about five hundred meters away from the tunnel and I heard the sound of the growling beast no more. I was happy that I was not captured by the beast.

Chapter Two: Angelic Intervention

As I sat down to rest for a while before continuing the race, I heard voices as of angels singing and making melodious sound. So I decided to wait and see from where this melodious sound was coming. Not more than five angels were approaching me with thorns and whips in their hands. I took to my heels again. Running for my life, I finally halted, I took out a little piece of writing from my pocket, I read *"Whosoever shall run, must run as he is alive"*. I took another piece of writing from my left pocket and read again "whosoever run, must run even before he starts running."

"And it came to pass, when they had brought them forth abroad, that he said, Escape for thy life; look not behind thee, neither stay thou in all the plain; escape to the mountain, lest thou be consumed."

Genesis 19:17.

The piece from my right pocket is contrary to that on my left pocket. At this I started weeping; I wept for a while and cleaned my eyes. Then I started hearing the humming of a little bird along the tunnel and away from it. I came closer to the bird but on coming closer, I looked and saw that the bird was not an ordinary bird. Inside the eyes of the bird was written *"they that fly shall conquer"*. I immediately imagined that I had wings to fly yet had I none. The thought of flying was strong on me, while the thought of running was very practical. I continued running, I ran as a deer but was not at all tired because what was on my sides were a spear and a shield which the **Lord Almighty** gave to me for greatness.

"Thou hast also given me the shield of thy salvation: and thy gentleness hath made me great." 2 Samuel 22: 36.

As I ran, from a distance to my front, I heard songs of angels. At this moment I decided not to take chances as earlier, so I decided to wait at that spot to know those passing by, if they were angels of light or of darkness? As I watched with keen interest, I heard a voice behind me saying *"son of man what doeth thou here"*. As I tried to recognize the voice talking to me, lo and behold! I saw a man with fingers like that of a lion and a head like that of an eagle. To identify him was unimaginable. As I wanted to shout, he quickly gave me a piece that I should chew.

"Moreover he said unto me, Son of man, eat that thou findest; eat this roll, and go speak unto the house of Israel." Ezekiel 3:1.

. As soon as I finished chewing, a giant stood in front of me and said *"Where are you going"*? I was about to speak when I heard the growling of the beast behind me. At this juncture, I remembered I had a piece which was given to me by the creature with the fingers of a lion and the face of an eagle. I quickly removed it from my left side pocket and tried to read quickly. Then I heard a voice in front of me saying *"don't do! don't do!! don't do!!!"*. In my attempt to recognize the face and the voice, I heard another voice telling me *"remember to fly just as the bird you saw along the tunnel"*. At this juncture, I started running, but the more I ran the more a negative force was pulling me backwards, so much that my speed was impeded. Then I wondered if I was running at all. The more I ran the more the force tries to draw me back.

"Now the just shall live by faith: but if any man draw back, My soul shall have no pleasure in him." Hebrews 10:38.

Chapter Three: The Rescue

As I was about to complain of the force pulling me back, a voice told me that "His grace is sufficient for you".

"And he said unto me, My grace is sufficient for thee: for My strength is made perfect in weakness. Most gladly therefore will I rather glory in my infirmities, that the power of Christ may rest upon me."2corinthians 12:9.

The creature that was before me tried to draw me out of the tunnel of destruction, while the one behind me tried to pull me into destruction. I started praying in my dialect *"Oh God what have I done, rescue me from this predicament"*. Immediately I finished praying, the creature took me away in the air.

"But they that wait upon the Lord shall renew their strength; they shall mount up with wings as eagles; they shall run, and not be weary; and they shall walk, and not faint."Isaiah 40:31.

As he flew with me, I wondered if I was in the dream or not, but he told me not to worry that he was sent by the Lord to rescue me from the tunnel of destruction.

"He shall cover thee with His feathers, and under His wings shalt thou trust: His truth shall be thy shield and buckler."Psalms 91:4.

The tunnel from where I was rescued was bedeviled by all forms of filthy creatures. The first creature is called "Abadidon" the queen of all the evil creatures in the tunnel. She was called the queen of all the evil creatures, because over the years she had succeeded in pulling men into the region of destruction with her flattery.

"To deliver thee from the strange woman, even from the stranger which flattereth with her words; which forsaketh the guide of her youth, and forgetteth the covenant of her God. For her house inclineth unto death, and her paths unto the dead. None that go unto her return again, neither take they hold of the paths of life."Proverbs 2:16-19.

With her much fair speech she had wounded men and with her ornaments she had seduced men into fornication. Her bed is always perfumed with myrrh and aloes. Her feet never stay within but she moves from street to street to get whom she will wound. Her victims (men) never live to tell the story.

"And, behold, there met him a woman with the attire of an harlot, and subtil of heart. (She is loud and stubborn; her feet abide not in her house: Now is she without, now in the streets, and lieth in wait at every corner.) So she caught him, and kissed him, and with an impudent face said unto him, I have peace offerings with me; this day have I payed my vows. Therefore came I forth to meet thee, diligently to seek thy face, and I have found thee. I have decked my bed with coverings of tapestry, with carved works, with fine linen of Egypt. I have perfumed

my bed with myrrh, aloes, and cinnamon. With her much fair speech she caused him to yield, with the flattering of her lips she forced him. He goeth after her straightway, as an ox goeth to the slaughter, or as a fool to the correction of the stocks; Till a dart strike through his liver; as a bird hasteth to the snare, and knoweth not that it is for his life. Hearken unto me now therefore, O ye children, and attend to the words of my mouth. Let not thine heart decline to her ways, go not astray in her paths. For she hath cast down many wounded: yea, many strong men have been slain by her. Her house is the way to hell, going down to the chambers of death."Proverbs 7:10-17; 21-27.

The creature sent by God, who had the fingers of a lion and the face of an eagle, was not at all an angel but a beast, hence, a holy beast.

"And before the throne there was a sea of glass like unto crystal: and in the midst of the throne, and round about the throne, were four beasts full of eyes before and behind. And the first beast was like a lion, and the second beast like a calf, and the third beast had a face as a man, and the fourth beast was like a flying eagle." Revelation 4:6-7.

In the sky, the beast told me that I was a **Jumper at the Gate of Hell,** which was why he was sent by the Most High to rescue me from that realm of destruction.

Chapter Four: Journey to the Kingdom of God

I had wanted to ask the beast what he meant by me being a **Jumper at the Gate of Hell** but he told me that I must enter the kingdom of God for him to tell me what that meant. As we soar in the sky, from a certain distance I heard voices of angels and saints from where we were. Their voices were like that of many waters and mighty thunderings.

"And I heard as it were the voice of a great multitude, and as the voice of many waters, and as the voice of mighty thunderings, saying, Alleluia: for the Lord God omnipotent reigneth." Revelation 19: 6.

When we arrived at the gate of heaven the angels and the saints welcomed me with a glorious welcome.

Creature: Brother Paul, why did you enter the tunnel of hell; don't you know that they that go into it hardly come out alive?

Me: It is good that God has allowed me to taste death knowing that the works of darkness are altogether unfruitful *"It is good for me that I have been afflicted; that I might learn Thy statutes." Psalms119:71.*

"And have no fellowship with the unfruitful works of darkness, but rather reprove them." Ephesians 5:11.

Angel 1: *"For God so loved the world, that He gave His only begotten Son, that whosoever believeth in Him should not perish, but have everlasting life." John 3:16.*

Angel 2: *"Now the just shall live by faith: but if any man draw back, My soul shall have no pleasure in him."Hebrews10:38; "The soul that sinneth, it shall die......"Ezekiel 18:20.*

Angel 3: *"Because that, when they knew God, they glorified Him not as God, neither were thankful; but became vain in their imaginations, and their foolish heart was darkened. Professing themselves to be wise, they became fools, And changed the glory of the uncorruptible God into an image made like to corruptible man, and to birds, and fourfooted beasts, and creeping things."Romans 1:21-23.*

Saint 1: They that shall overcome shall join us in singing to our God who has given us victory over the devil. *"And they sing the song of Moses the servant of God, and the song of the Lamb, saying, Great and marvellous are Thy works, Lord God Almighty; just and true are Thy ways, Thou King of saints." Revelation 15: 3.*

Saint 2: Have you not read that *"To him that overcometh will I give to eat of the hidden manna, and will give him a white stone, and in the stone a new name written, which no man knoweth saving he that receiveth it."Revelation 2: 17.*

Chapter Five: Conversation With the Patriarchs of old
(Abraham, Abel and Enoch)

Elder 1: I was tested by GOD yet I was given grace to pass the test. The Lord changed my name yet it was for a purpose but many have not allowed God to change their names. They did not give God the chance to change their names for once. One's name may signify evil but when a man comes in contact with God his name is changed for the better; from hardship to breakthrough, from the father of a son to the father of many Nations.

"And I will make My covenant between Me and thee, and will multiply thee exceedingly. And Abram fell on his face: and God talked with him, saying, As for Me, behold, My covenant is with thee, and thou shalt be a father of many nations. Neither shall thy name any more be called Abram, but thy name shall be Abraham; for a father of many nations have I made thee. This is My covenant, which ye shall keep, between Me and you and thy seed after thee; every man child among you shall be circumcised. And ye shall circumcise the flesh of your foreskin; and it shall be a token of the covenant betwixt Me and you. And he that is eight days old shall be circumcised among you, every man child in your generations, he that is born in the house, or bought with money of any stranger, which is not of thy seed. He that is born in thy house, and he that is bought with thy money, must needs be circumcised: and My covenant shall be in your flesh for an everlasting covenant." Genesis 17:2-5, 10-13.

God made a covenant with me to circumcise every male child born when I was on earth; but God has used His only Son (Christ) to circumcise the flesh. When the flesh is circumcised the things of the flesh is cut off, then the things of the Spirit begins to manifest in our lives.

"But the fruit of the Spirit is love, joy, peace, longsuffering, gentleness, goodness, faith, Meekness, temperance: against such there is no law. And they that are Christ's have crucified the flesh with the affections and lusts." Galatians 5:22-25.

God blessed me with a holy woman with whom I spent my life on earth, at an old age without a child yet I did not worry because of the love I had for her but many people cannot bear for a decade with their wife for not putting to birth. For God's love, my wife was also blessed, when her name was changed, things turned around for good in her life. At one hundred years I had a son, he was a miraculous child. At a hundred years old, I had an heir who would inherit all that God gave to me. The Lord put a smile on my face; I was named the father of a son and men celebrated with me.

"And the Lord visited Sarah as he had said, and the Lord did unto Sarah as he had spoken. For Sarah conceived, and bare Abraham a son in his old age, at the set time of which God had spoken to him. And Abraham was an hundred years old, when his son Isaac was born unto him. And Sarah said, God hath made me to laugh, so that all that hear will laugh with me. And

she said, Who would have said unto Abraham, that Sarah should have given children suck? For I have born him a son in his old age."Genesis 21:1-2, 5-7.

Elder 2: I was killed by my brother because of envy.

"But unto Cain and to his offering he had not respect. And Cain was very wroth, and his countenance fell. And Cain talked with Abel his brother: and it came to pass, when they were in the field, that Cain rose up against Abel his brother, and slew him." Genesis 4:5, 8.

"Wrath is cruel, and anger is outrageous; but who is able to stand before envy?" Proverbs 27: 4.

Those who are envious of other's success will not obtain goodness from God. *"For wrath killeth the foolish man, and envy slayeth the silly one." Job5:2.* Because of envy the chief priests and the Pharisees were looking for how to trap our Lord Jesus Christ in order for Him to be crucified.

A greedy man cannot enter into the kingdom of God because a greedy man cannot give and when he gives he gives from his waste. My brother gave from his waste, that was why his sacrifice was rejected, but I gave from my goodness (best) and that was why my sacrifice was accepted.

"By faith Abel offered unto God a more excellent sacrifice than Cain, by which he obtained witness that he was righteous,

God testifying of his gifts: and by it he being dead yet speaketh."Heb11:4.

Elder 3: Men on earth are still confused of my death. They searched for me here and there but could not find me. Some say I was translated and some are having doubts of my translation. I have to put on the celestial body while ascending by the power of the Holy Ghost.

"And Enoch walked with God: and he was not; for God took him."Genesis 5:24.

The mortality was displaced and the immortality was put on. Men said that my life pleased God but men have refused to please God with their lives. *"By faith Enoch was translated that he should not see death; and was not found, because God had translated him: for before his translation he had this testimony, that he pleased God." Hebrews11:5.*

Chapter Six: Conversation With the Patriarchs of old
(Noah, Isaac and Joseph)

Elder 4: In my generation, wickedness was great in the earth, and every imagination of the thoughts of men's heart was only evil continually. They were filled with evil thoughts of; cheating, murder and having sex with the same sex (Sodomy) just as it is in your generation today.

"And God saw that the wickedness of man was great in the earth, and that every imagination of the thoughts of his heart was only evil continually."Genesis 6:5.

Men removed God from their hearts and God wiped them away with flood. *"And spared not the old world, but saved Noah the eighth person, a preacher of righteousness, bringing in the flood upon the world of the ungodly;" 2 Peter 2:5* .

The wickedness of men made God to reduce his age to a hundred and twenty years.

"And the Lord said, My spirit shall not always strive with man, for that he also is flesh: yet his days shall be an hundred and twenty years."Genesis 6:3.

Elder 5: My father is the father of faith, and because of his love and fear for God; God made him the father of many nations. He gave his only son and in return God gave him children like the sand by the seashore. At an old age my father gave birth to me, which means God is never late.

"He hath made every thing beautiful in His time: also He hath set the world in their heart, so that no man can find out the work that God maketh from the beginning to the end." Ecclesiastes 3:11.

"For Sarah conceived, and bare Abraham a son in his old age, at the set time of which God had spoken to him. And Abraham was an hundred years old, when his son Isaac was born unto him." Genesis 21:2, 5.

He that believes in Him shall never be disappointed except if he is not deeply rooted in GOD.

Elder 6: I was the first Judge In the Land of Israel. I was loved by my father more than all his children and this made them sold me out into the hands of Ishmaelites. I had coat of many colors which was given to me by my father just as our Lord Jesus has given those living on earth salvation with many goodness.

"Now Israel loved Joseph more than all his children, because he was the son of his old age: and he made him a coat of many colours." GenESIS 37:3.

"I will greatly rejoice in the Lord, my soul shall be joyful in my God; for He hath clothed me with the garments of salvation, He hath covered me with the robe of righteousness, as a bridegroom decketh himself with ornaments, and as a bride adorneth herself with her jewels." Isaiah 61:10.

Had I yielded to the temptation of my master's wife then, you wouldn't have found me here in Heaven.

Chapter Seven: Conversation With the Patriarchs of Old
(Gideon, Jephthah and Prophet Samuel)

Elder 7: When I was on earth I was known as a mighty man of valor, yet I did not know until an angel of the most-high God told me.

"And there came an angel of the Lord, and sat under an oak which was in Ophrah, that pertained unto Joash the Abi-ezrite: and his son Gideon threshed wheat by the winepress, to hide it from the Midianites. And the angel of the Lord appeared unto him, and said unto him, The Lord is with thee, thou mighty man of valour."Juges 6:11-12.

Many believers are mighty men of valor, yet they shiver at small trials that come their way. *"I have said, Ye are gods; and all of you are children of the most High." Psalms 82:6.*

I also led men through the water at the instruction of the living God in order for Him to try them at the water. He told me to divide them into two groups according to how they drank the water. The first group was those that took the water in their hands to get it to their mouths and sipped it like dogs, while the second group was those who knelt down and drank with their mouths in the stream. Only three hundred men drank from their hands while the rest got down to their knees and drank with their mouths in the stream. The Lord told me with these three hundred men He would rescue the Israelites and give us victory over our enemies.

"And the Lord said unto Gideon, The people are yet too many; bring them down unto the water, and I will try them for

thee there: and it shall be, that of whom I say unto thee, This shall go with thee, the same shall go with thee; and of whomsoever I say unto thee, This shall not go with thee, the same shall not go. So he brought down the people unto the water: and the Lord said unto Gideon, Every one that lappeth of the water with his tongue, as a dog lappeth, him shalt thou set by himself; likewise every one that boweth down upon his knees to drink. And the number of them that lapped, putting their hand to their mouth, were three hundred men: but all the rest of the people bowed down upon their knees to drink water. And the Lord said unto Gideon, By the three hundred men that lapped will I save you, and deliver the Midianites into thine hand: and let all the other people go every man unto his place." Judges 7:4-7.

In your generation, men of God are called to serve God in holiness, righteousness and truth, but with the three hundred men (sheep) God will give to them (ministries) they will win souls for the kingdom of God. Millions of souls shall give their lives to Jesus.

Elder 8: I was also a mighty man of valor and I was the son of a harlot: I was thrust out by my half brothers and sisters. They thrust me out and said I will not partake in the inheritance of my father's house, because I was the son of a strange woman.

"Now Jephthah the Gileadite was a mighty man of valour, and he was the son of an harlot: and Gilead begat Jephthah. And

Gilead's wife bare him sons; and his wife's sons grew up, and they thrust out Jephthah, and said unto him, Thou shalt not inherit in our father's house; for thou art the son of a strange woman. Judges11:1-2.

But our God is a God of knowledge and by Him actions are weighed 1samuel 2:3.

God looked at me with his divine mercy and turned things around for my good by stirring war between Israel and Ammon. This made the Elders of Israel to search for me in order to be their captain in the war against Ammon. The war was for a purpose, God wanted to show men that the corner stone that was rejected will return to be the chief corner stone. The elders searched for me (an insignificant person) and presented their problems by asking me to go and fight for the children of Israel against the children of Ammon.

"And it came to pass in process of time, that the children of Ammon made war against Israel. And it was so, that when the children of Ammon made war against Israel, the elders of Gilead went to fetch Jephthah out of the land of Tob: And they said unto Jephthah, Come, and be our captain, that we may fight with the children of Ammon." Judges11:4-6.

Before I went for the war, I made a vow unto the Lord "......*and said, If Thou shalt without fail deliver the children of Ammon into mine hands, Then it shall be, that whatsoever cometh forth of the doors of my house to meet me, when I return in peace from the children of Ammon, shall surely be the Lord's, and I will offer it up for a burnt offering." Judges 11:30-31.*

Many people on earth wonder how a man can make such an expensive vow unto God, but it was the will of God for Him to put it into my heart, knowing that it was going to be for a purpose. My only child was the first thing that came out to meet me at my return from the war.

"And Jephthah came to Mizpeh unto his house, and, behold, his daughter came out to meet him with timbrels and with dances: and she was his only child; beside her he had neither son nor daughter. And it came to pass, when he saw her, that he rent his clothes, and said, Alas, my daughter! thou hast brought me very low, and thou art one of them that trouble me: for I have opened my mouth unto the Lord, and I cannot go back." Judges 11:34-35.

Elder 9: My father married my mother and another woman (he had two wives). My mother was God fearing but had no child while the second woman had children. The second woman was always mocking my mother, because she was barren. But my mother was greatly beloved by my father. My mother had to cry unto God before the altar and through the man of God. The lord visited my mother and after a year of the positive proclamation by the man of God, my mother gave birth to me. My mother also made vow before the altar which was inspired by the almighty God because it was by the will of

God she made that vow. It was a sacrificial vow before God - giving God back what He has given you.

Some people on earth are so greedy that after the blessings of God almighty in their lives they forget to give the one tenth of that blessing. My mother did not give one-tenth but she gave tenth of tenth (all completely).

"For this child I prayed; and the Lord hath given me my petition which I asked of him: Therefore also I have lent him to the Lord; as long as he liveth he shall be lent to the Lord. And he worshipped the Lord there."1 Samuel 1:27-28.

As a result of what she did, the Lord visited her again and gave her sons and daughters.

"And the Lord visited Hannah, so that she conceived, and bare three sons and two daughters. And the child Samuel grew before the Lord." 1 Samuel 2:21.

As for me, the Lord made me a great prophet under the surface of the earth. He started using me at a very young age.

"And the child Samuel ministered unto the Lord before Eli. And the word of the Lord was precious in those days; there was no open vision. And Samuel grew, and the Lord was with him, and did let none of his words fall to the ground. And all Israel from Dan even to Beer-sheba knew that Samuel was established to be a prophet of the Lord."1Samuel 3:1, 19-20.

Many people in your generation have allowed the devil to deceive them by making them feel they are too young to serve God Almighty. Have they forgotten what is written in the New Testament that:

"......I write unto you, young men, because ye have overcome the wicked one. I write unto you, little children, because ye have known the Father." 1 John 2:13.

The young ones have overcome the wicked one. The young ones have the strength to go from one end of the world unto another for evangelism without undue tiredness. The young ones have the strength to work in the vineyard of the Lord by the Help of the Holy Ghost. The young ones have the strength to organize programs here and there by the help of the Holy Ghost. The young ones have the strength to go from one house to another for house visitation, with that, members have the feelings that they are cared for. Brother Paul, you are also young hence you have overcome the wicked one. But due to your carelessness, you almost allowed the wicked one to overcome you if not for the timely intervention of our Lord Jesus by sending one of His Holy beast to rescue you from the tunnel of hell. Many youths on earth are in this tunnel of hell because of carelessness and the deceit of the devil. Most are unlucky and die on earth along this tunnel and immediately they die, they find themselves along this tunnel and when they find themselves along this tunnel after death, it becomes too late for them.

"And as it is appointed unto men once to die, but after this the judgment:" Hebrews 9:27.

But thank God you were timely rescued because it was the divine will of God that you be a jumper at the gate of hell.

Me: Sir, what do you mean by I am a Jumper at the Gate of Hell?

Elder 10: You will soon know what that means. The next elder wants to talk with you.

Chapter Eight: Conversation With the Patriarchs of Old
(David, Obededom, Hezekiah and Ezra)

Elder 11: I am the son of the Son of God. Most people call me the bravest of all kings in Israel. Yet I was brave because He who is in me is the Lion of the tribe of Judah.

"Ye are of God, little children, and have overcome them: because greater is He that is in you, than he that is in the world." 1John 4:4.

I fought with a giant on earth and I prevailed over him with the instrument God gave to me.

"So David prevailed over the Philistine with a sling and with a stone, and smote the Philistine, and slew him...." 1Samuel 17:50.

Through his death I was known in the land of Israel. God Almighty used women to make me famous in Israel because of the song they sang on my return from the war. *"And it came to pass as they came, when David was returned from the slaughter of the Philistine, that the women came out of all cities of Israel, singing and dancing, to meet king Saul, with tabrets, with joy, and with instruments of musick. And the women answered one another as they played, and said, Saul hath slain his thousands, and David his ten thousands." 1Samuel 18:6-7.*

I was the least in my father's house but for God's mercies, I was lifted above my brethren.

"Then Samuel took the horn of oil, and anointed him in the midst of his brethren: and the Spirit of the Lord came upon David from that day forward. So Samuel rose up, and went to Ramah." 1Samuel 16:13.

I was called the man after God's heart because God has called me the man after His own Heart. Yet in your generation I am yet to see the man after God's heart.

Elder 12: I am highly favored by the blessings of God. Within three months of an encounter with God, the Lord made the children of Israel to talk about the blessings of God to the king that he had to bring back that which brought my break through into his house. Within three months, God turned my sadness to joy, my demotion to promotion, and my unyielding field into a very fertile field that my herds and crops were multiplied within these three months of the presence of God in my house.

"And the ark of God remained with the family of Obed-edom in his house three months. And the Lord blessed the house of Obed-edom, and all that he had." 1Chronicles 13:14.

Elder 13: When I was on earth, a prophesy was given to me when I was sick that I would die. But due to my zeal for the Lord I challenged the Lord by telling Him to remember now how I have walked before Him in truth and with a perfect heart and have done that which was good in His sight.

"In those days was Hezekiah sick unto death. And Isaiah the prophet the son of Amoz came unto him, and said unto him, Thus saith the Lord, Set thine house in order: for thou shalt die, and not live. Then Hezekiah turned his face toward the wall, and prayed unto the Lord, And said, Remember now, O Lord, I beseech thee, how I have walked before Thee in truth and with a perfect heart, and have done that which is good in Thy sight. And Hezekiah wept sore. Then came the word of the Lord to Isaiah, saying, Go, and say to Hezekiah, Thus saith the Lord, the God of David thy father, I have heard thy prayer, I have seen thy tears: behold, I will add unto thy days fifteen years." Isaiah 38:1-5.

To Believers who worship God in spirit and in truth, there are things that are not meant to come their way. And when it does, you challenge God by telling Him "Lord your word say so… and so…and I am standing on the word which is living and proclaiming that this… and that…will not happen again in my family place and business" and the everlasting Father will perfect His words on that positive proclamation. For my faithfulness on earth, the Lord added fifteen years to my life.

Brother Paul, in this your generation, men who are blessed by God are still eating that which belongs to God. Some are millionaires, some are billionaires, some are even trillionaires, yet before God they are the thieves and armed robbers of His kingdom. Do you know why they are called armed robbers? They are called armed robbers because they use their alms (refusal to pay their tithe/disobedience) in robbing the everlasting God that has given them all the goodness. Although some of them are armed robbers on earth and after stealing (through their offices- embezzling government funds), they bring the one tenth of the money as tithes - this is an abomination. They collect the blessings of others and come before God almighty to present it as a sacrifice. It is just as Cain's sacrifice before the MOST HIGH GOD.

"A son honoureth his father, and a servant his master: if then I be a Father, where is Mine honour? and if I be a Master, where is My fear? saith the Lord of hosts unto you, O priests, that despise My name. And ye say, Wherein have we despised Thy name? Ye offer polluted bread upon Mine altar; and ye say, Wherein have we polluted Thee? In that ye say, The table of the Lord is contemptible. And if ye offer the blind for sacrifice, is it not evil? and if ye offer the lame and sick, is it not evil? offer it now unto thy governor; will he be pleased with thee, or accept thy person? saith the Lord of hosts.And now, I pray you, beseech God that He will be gracious unto us: this hath been by your means: will He regard your persons? saith the Lord of hosts. Malacchi 1:6-9.

Elder 14: When I was on earth, I was a scribe in the land of Israel. I was from the lineage of Aaron the high priest. I came out from

Babylon where we were in captivity. The king released me and granted my entire request according to the hand of the Lord upon me. For I have prepared my heart to seek the law of the Lord, and to do it, and to teach in Israel statutes and judgments. The Lord God of heaven put it into the king's heart to release me and other workers in the vineyard of GOD in order to beautify the house of the LORD in Jerusalem.

"Now after these things, in the reign of Artaxerxes king of Persia, Ezra the son of Seraiah, the son of Azariah, the son of Hilkiah. This Ezra went up from Babylon; and he was a ready scribe in the law of Moses, which the Lord God of Israel had given: and the king granted him all his request, according to the hand of the Lord his God upon him. For Ezra had prepared his heart to seek the law of the Lord, and to do it, and to teach in Israel statutes and judgments." Ezra7:1, 6,10.

But when I came to Jerusalem I learnt that the people did not separate themselves from the people of the lands, doing according to their abominations, even of the Canaanites, the Hittites, the Perizzites, the Jebusites, the Ammonites, the Moabites, the Egyptians, and the Amorites. For they took their daughters for themselves, and for their sons: so that the holy seed have mingled themselves with the people of those lands.

"And among the sons of the priests there were found that had taken strange wives: namely, of the sons of Jeshua the son

of Jozadak, and his brethren; Maaseiah, and Eliezer, and Jarib, and Gedaliah. All these had taken strange wives: and some of them had wives by whom they had children." Ezra10:18, 44.

Brother Paul, likewise in your generation the daughters of Zion have mingled themselves with worldly husbands because of impatience for their rightful life partners and when the daughters of Zion marries sinners, there is every tendencies that the worldly man will pull them back into sin.

"Neither shalt thou make marriages with them; thy daughter thou shalt not give unto his son, nor his daughter shalt thou take unto thy son. For they will turn away thy son from following me, that they may serve other gods: so will the anger of the Lord be kindled against you, and destroy thee suddenly." Deuteronomy 7:3-4.

Not only to the daughters of Zion do these things happen to, but also to men of God who are impatient and because of physical beauty they marry a woman (daughter of Egypt) who is not their correct life partner. So therefore, the work of God suffers because of these women. The man of God cannot preach on outward holiness because his wife is also putting the Egyptian adornment on her body. For that reason, the man of God whom God has given a holy ministry is forced to change his ministry to a worldly ministry because of the outward dressing of his wife.

"Did not Solomon king of Israel sin by these things? yet among many nations was there no king like him, who was beloved of his God, and God made him king over all Israel: nevertheless even him did outlandish women cause to sin."
Nehemiah 13:26.

Brother Paul, many and many great men of God that are on earth now are called by God and were given holy ministries but some because of the love for money, they have refused to preach the true gospel to the sheep God has given to them. This they do because they don't want to offend the members of the church with the true gospel and as such they dilute the message God has put into their hearts in order not to offend the members of their churches. Brother Paul, when you go back, tell them that the most high God is waiting for them at the throne of judgment because they have wasted a lot of souls that should have entered the kingdom of God, but because of their outward dressing they are defiled and polluted before God.

Brother Paul, tell them that their dressing matters because if God would curse man on earth for eating the forbidden fruit (disobedience) which He told him not to eat and he did, how much more the Egyptian properties?

"And when the people heard these evil tidings, they mourned: and no man did put on him his ornaments. For the Lord had said unto Moses, Say unto the children of Israel, Ye are a stiffnecked people: I will come up into the midst of thee in

a moment, and consume thee: therefore now put off thy ornaments from thee, that I may know what to do unto thee. And the children of Israel stripped themselves of their ornaments by the mount Horeb."Exodus 33:4-6

"In like manner also, that women adorn themselves in modest apparel, with shamefacedness and sobriety; not with broided hair, or

gold, or pearls, or costly array;" 1 Timothy 2:9.

Chapter Nine: Angels Lament

Angel 4: If men know that God is interested in both their inward and outward holiness they will not gamble with their lives on earth. *"Having therefore these promises, dearly beloved, let us cleanse ourselves from all filthiness of the flesh and spirit, perfecting holiness in the fear of God." 2Cor7:1.*

"Who shall ascend into the hill of the Lord? or who shall stand in his holy place? He that hath clean hands, and a pure heart; who hath not lifted up his soul unto vanity, nor sworn deceitfully. Psalm 24:3-4

"Blessed are the pure in heart: for they shall see God." Matthew 5:8.

Brother Paul: Men and women on earth are sometimes given grace; the Lord Jesus takes them to heaven and hell to show them the mysteries of heaven and the destruction of hell. However, many souls of men have counteracted this, saying that "it is a false Jesus that is appearing to them". I was also among these ones that counteracted these divine revelations but thank God that I was rescued by the Holy beast. It would have been too late for me to believe after death.

"Take heed, brethren, lest there be in any of you an evil heart of unbelief, in departing from the living God." Hebrews 3:12.

Angel 5: Brother Paul, even when you return to the world and tell them of the mysteries your eyes have beheld, they will still doubt you. Men will not belief until they have seen hell with their two eyes, and by that time, it would have been too late for them. No matter what they say at the throne of God, it will not stop the stormy wind from sweeping them into the region of darkness, where they shall burn forever and ever weeping and gnashing their teeth where their worms shall never die.

Chapter Ten: Conversation With the Patriarchs of Old
(Nehemiah, Job and Isaiah)

Elder 15: I was in the king's palace during the captivity in Babylon, when I heard a disheartening message concerning my people that the remnants that were left of the captivity are in great affliction and reproach. When I heard these words, I sat down and wept, and mourned certain days, and fasted, and prayed before the God of heaven.

"And they said unto me, The remnant that are left of the captivity there in the province are in great affliction and reproach: the wall of Jerusalem also is broken down, and the gates thereof are burned with fire. And it came to pass, when I heard these words, that I sat down and wept, and mourned certain days, and fasted, and prayed before the God of heaven."Nehemiah1:3-4.

Brother Paul in this your generation there are men and women who fast and pray for many days by the leading of the Holy Ghost for the world to experience peace. Yet there are those on earth who have become the devil's tool and the devil uses them any time he wants to cause havoc on earth. Some of them are; suicide bombers, rapist, armed robbers, false prophets, false teachers, terrorist, while some beliefs by killing themselves and others they will enter into the kingdom of God. All these are devices of the devil to cause confusion on humanity upon the earth. When they die, he (the devil) will begin to torment them in the pit of hell.

Elder 16: Brother Paul, people on earth often use my predicament on earth as joke. When they see people suffering they will ask, why is the person suffering like me? Some would say, that their suffering is more than mine. But God knows, if He should allow one-tenth of what befell me on earth on these ones, they will curse God and commit suicide. I was loved by God almighty because I was upright before Him. Yet the uprightness was not of me, it was the gift of God. I had love and fear for God which is the righteousness of God. That was why He reckoned me to be righteous before Him.

"And the Lord said unto Satan, Hast thou considered My servant Job, that there is none like him in the earth, a perfect and an upright man, one that feareth God, and escheweth evil?" Job1:8.

During my temptation on earth, I had a worldly woman whom I married; this woman almost drew me into everlasting destruction if not for the grace of God.

"Then said his wife unto him, Dost thou still retain thine integrity? curse God, and die." Job 2:9.

Brother Paul, tell believers on earth to be patient for their life partners. They should attain a high level of spirituality in order to be able to hear from God, whether the person they are going to marry is their divine partner or not. A lot of believers have made mistakes in choosing the wrong life partners because of impatience. Some because of physical beauty they married the wrong woman into their family; she becomes a thorn in the flesh of the husband and the husbands family. The woman I married on earth almost made me sin against God if not for the grace of God in my life.

Elder 17: I was also a great prophet in Israel, by the power of God I predicted the Messiah that was coming to redeem men on earth, which has occurred and salvation is free unto all men that are willing to accept the Son of man into their lives.

"For unto us a Child is born, unto us a Son is given: and the government shall be upon His shoulder: and His name shall be called Wonderful, Counsellor, The mighty God, The everlasting Father, The Prince of Peace. Of the increase of His government and peace there shall be no end, upon the throne of David, and upon His kingdom, to order it, and to establish it with judgment and with justice from henceforth even forever. The zeal of the Lord of hosts will perform this." Isaiah 9:6-7.

I was also privileged to be among the few that were able to see the mysteries beyond when I was on earth unlike your day, when men have turned these mysteries into a mockery. They mock those God has given special grace in these last days, those He has taken to heaven and hell in order to warn humanity about the danger that will befall them if they die without accepting Jesus.

"In the year that king Uzziah died I saw also the Lord sitting upon a throne, high and lifted up, and His train filled the temple. Above it stood the seraphims: each one had six wings; with twain he covered his face, and with twain he covered his feet, and with twain he did fly. And one cried unto another, and said, Holy, holy, holy, is the Lord of hosts: the whole earth is full of His glory. And the posts of the door moved at the voice of him that cried, and the house was filled with smoke. Then said I, Woe is me! for I am undone; because I am a man of unclean lips, and I dwell in the midst of a people of unclean lips: for mine eyes have seen the King, the Lord of hosts." Isaiah 6:1-5.

Also, those who have accepted Him but are still finding it difficult to do away with the Egyptian property; they put worldly things on their bodies and claim to be Christians. They use things that defile their garments before God and claim to be Christians. Brother Paul, when you go back to the world, tell them our God is a holy God. Anything that defiles or makes a lie cannot enter His presence.

"And there shall in no wise enter into it any thing that defileth, neither whatsoever worketh abomination, or maketh a lie: but they which are written in the Lamb's book of life." Revevelation 21: 27.

Women with artificial hair instead of their natural hair lie through such hairs. Women with artificial finger nails instead of their God given finger nails lie through such fingers. Women that apply cortex on their God given fingers lie through such material. Women who put on trousers lie about their gender. Women that walk seductively (cat-walk) in order to attract men are liars before God. Women that change their natural eye lashes, lie with such eyelashes. Women who change their genital organs (transgender) lie with their genital organs. Also men that perm their hair lie through such hairs. Men who change their genital organs (transgender) lie through such genital organ.

Brother Paul, do you know that men are putting on skirts on earth just like woman are putting on trousers? Men who put on skirt lie about their gender. Men with bleached skin are liars before God. Men that cover their natural teeth with gold are liars before God. Men that walk seductively in order to attract women or men are liars before God. All liars shall have their part in the lake of fire, where their worms shall never die.

Brother Paul, God is not a respecter of any man. Hence, whosoever that does these things may be a Bishop, Bishop's wife, Pastor, Pastor's wife, Prophet, Prophet's wife, Evangelist, Evangelist's wife, Apostle, Apostle's wife. Will never, never enter into the kingdom of God!

Chapter Eleven: The Name Above All Names

"Wherefore God also hath highly exalted Him, and given Him a name which is above every name: That at the name of Jesus every knee should bow, of things in heaven, and things in earth, and things under the earth; And that every tongue should confess that Jesus Christ is Lord, to the glory of God the Father." Philipians 2:9-11.

Angel 6: Brother Paul, you are a very privileged man on the surface of the earth. Only few are given this privilege. We the angels of the most high God are envious (holy envy) of human beings because God so loved humanity that He gave His only Son to die for the sins of the world.

"Of which salvation the prophets have inquired and searched diligently, who prophesied of the grace that should come unto you: Searching what, or what manner of time the Spirit of Christ which was in them did signify, when it testified beforehand the sufferings of Christ, and the glory that should follow. Unto whom it was revealed, that not unto themselves, but unto us they did minister the things, which are now reported unto you by them that have preached the gospel unto you with the Holy Ghost sent down from heaven; which things the angels desire to look into." 1 Peter 1:10-12.

Not only that, human beings have choice (permissive will), but we(Angels) do not have choice (self-will). Also, we were created in God's image but not in his likeness unlike human beings that are created in the image and likeness of God. Then if God created humanity in his image and likeness then why is humanity allowing the devil to use them by changing the likeness of God in them through; painting, putting of attachments, changing of genital organs, changing of the skin through bleaching. Human beings are privileged, yet humanity allowed the devil to deceive them to offend God through their outward dressing.

Angel 7: Brother Paul, haven't you read from the Holy Scriptures that

"Out of the mouth of babes and sucklings hast thou ordained strength because of thine enemies, that thou mightest still the enemy and the avenger." Psalms 8:2.

God so loved humanity and from their mouths (born again) He has ordained strength. Brother Paul, do you *know what that means?*

Me: How can I know unless you tell me?

Angel 7: It means that through the death of our Lord Jesus, you (believers) have victory over the devil at the mention of that name Jesus.

"That at the name of Jesus every knee should bow, of things in heaven, and things in earth, and things under the earth; And

that every tongue should confess that Jesus Christ is Lord, to the glory of God the Father." Philippians 2:10-11.

Angel 8: Any believer who mentions that name in the dream, physically or in the kingdom of darkness and nothing happens should go back to the altar for total repentance. *"The name of the Lord is a strong tower: the righteous runneth into it, and is safe." Proverbs18:10.*

Angel 9: Men on earth do not fully know the power behind that name although evil men knows, hence, before they(evil men) invoke their victims they usually make them dumb so that they won't have the strength to mention the name of the Son of God. Therefore their victims are invoked and stabbed in their demonic mirrors. The Son of God always sees these evil men and sometimes allows them to stab their victims who are still sinners. The reason for which Son of God sometimes allow the evil men is because His blood which He shed on the cross of Calvary can only protect His children, but these ones will go into the pit of hell because of their sins.

"He that committeth sin is of the devil; for the devil sinneth from the beginning. For this purpose the Son of God was manifested, that He might destroy the works of the devil. We know that whosoever is born of God sinneth not; but he that is begotten of God keepeth himself, and that wicked one toucheth him not." 1John3:8; 5:18.

They rejected Christ and did not accept His salvation into their lives while they are living. They did not hearken to the saving gospel. When they were alive their eyes were on the things of the world which are; the lust of the flesh and the lust of the eyes. They have redness of eyes which is the sinners' eyes. **"….who hath redness of eyes?" Proverbs 23: 29.** The eyes of sinner's are usually red; they are only attracted to the things of this world. They don't savor the things of God. Their eyes are always on pornography, their eyes are always on other people's life partners (adultery).

"Having eyes full of adultery, and that cannot cease from sin; beguiling unstable souls: an heart they have exercised with covetous practices; cursed children." 2 Peter 2:14.

Their eyes are always on other people's wealth, their eyes are always on how to make quick money and in the process they find themselves in secret cults.

Chapter Twelve: Conversation With the Patriarchs of Old
(Jeremiah)

Elder 18: I am also one of the great prophets under the surface of the earth. Then on earth, the word of the Lord came unto me saying; ***"Before I formed thee in the belly I knew thee; and before thou camest forth out of the womb I sanctified thee, and I ordained thee a prophet unto the nations. Then the Lord put forth his hand, and touched my mouth. And the Lord said unto me, Behold, I have put my words in thy mouth." Jeremiah 1:5, 9.***

Brother Paul, what a mighty God we serve. God Almighty told me that before He formed me in my mother's womby (lowest part of the earth) ***"My substance was not hid from thee, when I was made in secret, and curiously wrought in the lowest parts of the earth." Psalms 139:15.***

My substance (who I will be/my destiny) was not hid from God, when I was made in secret, and curiously wrought in the lowest parts (belly) of the earth. Brother Paul do you know what it means by we were curiously wrought? Go to the potter's house and see how he is working at his wheel. A porter who is working on a clay has in mind the things he wants to produce, but as he is molding the vessel he is really curious of seeing the finished product even though he has in mind the picture of the vessel. Brother Paul, do you know that you are perfect in the way God almighty created you? You are wonderfully made beneath the deep. It was at the deep that you were wonderfully made.

"I will praise thee; for I am fearfully and wonderfully made: marvellous are thy works; and that my soul knoweth right well. My substance was not hid from thee, when I was made in secret, and curiously wrought in the lowest parts of the earth."Psalms139:14-15. Do you remember Hannah's prayer? It says;

"…..For the pillars of the earth are the Lord's, and He hath set the world upon them."1Samuel 2:8.

Now, if you look at the prayer of Hannah which was put into her heart to pray by God, you will observe that the pillars holding the earth are the everlasting God Himself. Humanity was formed at the belly of the earth, and that this pillar (the everlasting God) goes beyond the earth and the world is placed upon this same pillar (the everlasting God). It means that the earth comes before the world, and you (man) was created in the lowest parts of the earth. Brother Paul it means that humanity existed even before the world was created. It is a mystery that you have been in existence even before the foundation of the world. That was why when God was talking to me, He said before He formed me in the belly (hearts of earth /deep) He knew me.

"And the Lord God formed man of the dust of the ground, and breathed into his nostrils the breath of life; and man became a living soul." *Genesis 2:7.*

Just like a potter has in mind of what he wants to create. God also said that before I came forth out of the womb (heaven) He sanctified me. After the death of Christ, paradise was moved from the deep to heaven and the things in heaven were sanctified by the blood of Jesus. That was why when Moses the servant of God was on earth he was commanded by God almighty concerning the things inside the tabernacle which signifies heaven. Therefore, if things of the tabernacle were sanctified by the sprinkling of blood of goats likewise things in heaven are also sanctified.

"For when Moses had spoken every precept to all the people according to the law, he took the blood of calves and of goats, with water, and scarlet wool, and hyssop, and sprinkled both the book, and all the people, Saying, This is the blood of the testament which God hath enjoined unto you. Moreover he sprinkled with blood both the tabernacle, and all the vessels of the ministry. And almost all things are by the law purged with blood; and without shedding of blood is no remission. It was therefore necessary that the patterns of things in the heavens should be purified with these; but the heavenly things themselves with better sacrifices than these. For Christ is not entered into the holy places made with hands, which are the figures of the true; but into heaven itself, now to appear in the presence of God for us." Hebrews 9:19-24.

As it is in heaven so it is on earth. Things in heaven became sanctified by the blood of Jesus after His death and resurrection. Therefore, Brother Paul before you came forth out of the womb (heaven) you have already been sanctified by the blood of Jesus. Although mine was by the power of the holy ghost because then the Lord Jesus had not died.

Chapter Thirteen: The Narrow Way

Angel 10: Brother Paul, if human beings know the way God created and loved them they will not put on anything artificial on their body. Where was lipstick when God was creating them in the deep? Where was cortex when God was creating them in the deep? Where was attachment when God was creating them in the deep? Nevertheless, the foolishness of man has permitted the devil to trick him into changing and distorting the wonderful creation of God. The devil knows that once human beings put on these artificial things on their body they will be distorted and polluted before God. Therefore, what they are indirectly telling the all wise God is that when he was creating them in the deep, he forgot to make them white.

"Woe unto him that striveth with his Maker! Let the potsherd strive with the potsherds of the earth. Shall the clay say to Him that fashioneth it, What makest thou? or thy work, He hath no hands?" Isaiah 45:9.

Angel 11: [singing]: Hallelujah, Hallelujah, Hallelujah, Hallelujah, Hallelujah, Hallelujah!

Me: I think I have heard this kind of song on earth. It sounds like a song I know.

Angel 10: That Angel is singing the Anthem of the kingdom of God. On earth there are all forms of anthems; National anthem, Institutional anthem and many more. Likewise in heaven this is the anthem of the saints and angels. The Angel is also singing because He knows that the coming of the Lord Jesus Christ on earth in order to take his bride home is at hand (the Rapture). Angels in charge of decorating believers' garments shall soon stop, at the shout of an archangel and the trump of God.

"For the Lord Himself shall descend from heaven with a shout, with the voice of the archangel, and with the trump of God: and the dead in Christ shall rise first: Then we which are alive and remain shall be caught up together with them in the clouds, to meet the Lord in the air: and so shall we ever be with the Lord." 1 Thessalonians 4:16-17.

Angel 12: They that shall fly shall conquer. Brother Paul, do you remember the bird you saw along the tunnel of hell? There are people on earth that are filled with the Holy Ghost, that along the narrow spiritual road they are neither running nor walking, but these ones are flying. They are flying not because they are too spiritual. No, they are flying because God almighty wants them to be in his presence whether the devil likes it or not. These ones (very few) are so filled with the Holy Ghost that they cannot do things on their own. They cannot pray on their own because anytime they open their mouths to pray even if they want to pray in their language, immediately they are opening their mouths the Holy Ghost gives them utterances to pray in tongues. They are so filled with the Holy Ghost that even if they close their mouth like Hannah, yet their spirits prays. *"Likewise the*

Spirit also helpeth our infirmities: for we know not what we should pray for as we ought: but the Spirit Itself maketh intercession for us with groanings which cannot be uttered." Romans 8:26.

They are so filled with the Holy Ghost that from their heart the Holy Ghost talk with them and they hear Him audibly. As the Holy Ghost is speaking in their hearts, the word is sanctifying them. Those that fly along the narrow road are so filled with the Holy Ghost to the extent that HE tells them what to do; the clothes that is good for them, the shoes that is good for them, places to go and where not to go. They hear Him audibly from their hearts. If they are travelling, He tells them things to carry and if they are about to go and have forgotten anything, He will remind them by putting it into their consciousness.

"But the Comforter, which is the Holy Ghost, whom the Father will send in My name, He shall teach you all things, and bring all things to your remembrance, whatsoever I have said unto you." John 14:26.

Chapter Fourteen: Conversation With the Patriarchs of Old
(Ezekiel)

Elder 19: I am also one of the great prophets on earth, in my generation.

"The hand of the Lord was upon me, and carried me out in the Spirit of the Lord, and set me down in the midst of the valley which was full of bones, And caused me to pass by them round about: and, behold, there were very many in the open valley; and, lo, they were very dry.

And He said unto me, Son of man, can these bones live? And I answered, O Lord God, thou knowest. Again He said unto me, Prophesy upon these bones, and say unto them, O ye dry bones, hear the word of the Lord. Thus saith the Lord God unto these bones; Behold, I will cause breath to enter into you, and ye shall live: And I will lay sinews upon you, and will bring up flesh upon you, and cover you with skin, and put breath in you, and ye shall live; and ye shall know that I am the Lord. So I prophesied as I was commanded: and as I prophesied, there was a noise, and behold a shaking, and the bones came together, bone to his bone. And when I beheld, lo, the sinews and the flesh came up upon them, and the skin covered them above: but there was no breath in them. Then said He unto me, Prophesy unto the wind, prophesy, son of man, and say to the wind, Thus saith the Lord God; Come from the four winds, O breath, and breathe upon these slain, that they may live. So I prophesied as He commanded me, and the breath came into them, and they lived, and stood up upon their feet, an exceeding great army." Ezekiel 37:1-10.

Brother Paul, do you know what these things mean?

Me: If you tell me I will be enlightened in the eternal reality of God's Glorious Gospel.

Elder 19: Brother Paul, the LORD carried me out in the spirit and set me down in the midst of the valley which was full of bones. Brother Paul, valley here means those that are still in the flesh, hence, living in sin and darkness. Those that have not experience the transforming power of the Lord Jesus.

Believers are on the mountain, and this mountain is our Lord Jesus Christ. Christian women are called daughters of Zion because they are standing on the mountain-and that is Jesus Christ. Therefore sinners are in the valley while believers are on the mountain. So, the Lord set me down in the midst of those living in sin; fornication, masturbation, adultery, sodomy, lies, gossip and many other satanic devices - the valley was full of dry bones.

The condition of these bones (sinners) was known to God, He therefore carried me into their midst so that they too would experience the glorious life of God. Brother Paul, the Lord caused me to pass by these bones (filthiness of the sinners) round about. It means by the help of the Holy Ghost, I was given the divine grace strength to go round every nook and cranny where these sinners were living. Behold they were many in the open valley. These sinners were much in numbers. Those living in this filthiness were much too, and lo they were very dry. Brother Paul the bones were very dry. They were living in acute filthiness and they needed urgent attention before it becomes late for them. So the everlasting Father asked me if these bones(sinners living in acute filthiness) can live?

Jehovah wanted me to give these sinners hope and faith (For Spirit works with the heart unlike human beings that work with the mouth). If the Spirit tells man to do something and he agrees to do it with joy and enthusiasm in reality, what the Spirit does is that (He does not take what the person has spoke from his lips), He searches the person's heart to see if it is in agreement with the utterances.

"And He that searcheth the hearts knoweth what is the mind of the Spirit, because He maketh intercession for the saints according to the will of God." Romans 8:27.

"The heart is deceitful above all things, and desperately wicked: who can know it? I the Lord search the heart, I try the reins, even to give every man according to his ways, and according to the fruit of his doings".Jeremiah17: 9-10.

If the person's heart is not saying the same thing with the mouth, then the Spirit will send leanness into his soul.

"But lusted exceedingly in the wilderness, and tempted God in the desert. And He gave them their request; but sent leanness into their soul." **Psalms 106:14-15.**

If Man knows what it means for God to send leanness into his soul, he will fear God. This is also the situation in churches whenever the preacher finishes preaching and makes an altar call; you will see multitudes coming out. They (most) are coming out not because they are convicted of their sins, but because they want to impress the man of God. Hence, their mouth is saying that "I surrender" while their hearts have not surrendered. Immediately the Spirit searches them and sees that their heart is speaking differently, He sends leanness to their souls and that is why you see such people can never be regenerated even if they respond to altar calls for salvation. It takes a special mercy from God for these ones (hypocrites) to be convicted by the Holy Spirit.

The Lord asked me if those dry bones (sinners living in extreme filthiness) can live? Hence, I was given grace by the same Spirit not to answer lest I answer and leanness is sent unto my soul. Then the Spirit caused me to say "O Lord God thou knowest". Eventually, the Lord gave these dry bones (sinners) hope in Himself by commanding me to prophesy upon the bones(sinners) and say unto them, "O ye dry bones, hear the word of the Lord. Thus saith the Lord God unto these bones (sinners), behold I will cause breath (salvation/ light) to enter into you(sinners) and you (sinners) shall know that I am the Lord".

Brother Paul, some evangelist never gave those they are evangelizing hope by proclaiming the gospel (good news) to them thereby giving them the faith they need. Brother Paul, I prophesied as the Lord commanded me unto those dry bones. I preached to those who loved fornication to depart from it because of the wrath of God that was imminent, I told those who loved drunkenness to depart from drunkenness. I told those who were homosexuals, just as it is in your generation to depart from homosexuality. I told prostitutes to depart from their whoredom. I told thieves to depart from their evils. As I preached to those living in the valley of sins, there was a noise (Conviction/weeping for repentance) and behold a shaking (shivering for repentance) and the bones came together (gradual transformation). And when I beheld, lo, the sinews (spiritual strength) and the flesh came up upon them (transformation) and the skin covered them above (God's purposes in their life) but there was no breath (The word of God). Then said he unto me prophesy unto the wind (teach them the word of God) prophesy son of man and say to the wind (by faith teach them the word of God), thus saith the Lord God, come from the four winds(by faith teach them the word of God in season and out of season). Brother Paul there are twelve months in a year; three months makes a quarter of the year. Hence there are four quarters in a year. I taught them the word of God all through these four quarters of the year (in season and out of season). O breath, breath upon these slain (converts), that they may live (have eternal life). So, I prophesied (taught the word of God) as He commanded me and breath(the word of God) came into them(their hearts) and they lived, and stood up upon their feet (they haven been converted by the word, also went out and preached /evangelized to others in darkness) , an exceeding great army (the soldiers of the cross).

Chapter Fifteen: Conversation With the Patriarchs of Old
(Malachi, Jonah and Micah)

Angel 13: Brother Paul, you are a favored man. Men on earth, especially men of knowledge (scholars) cannot comprehend the wisdom of God embedded in the word of God.

"In that hour Jesus rejoiced in spirit, and said, I thank thee, O Father, Lord of heaven and earth, that Thou hast hid these things from the wise and prudent, and hast revealed them unto babes: even so, Father; for so it seemed good in Thy sight." Luke 10:21.

Howbeit, men of wisdom (very few) by the power of the Holy Ghost are able to know the wisdom hidden in His word. When God tells a man " A" , a man of knowledge takes it as " A" but a man of wisdom by the power of the Holy Ghost sees eternity in that " A" . The word of God is eternal, hence should be understood by the inspired wisdom of the Holy Ghost.

Elder 20: I am also a prophet, a great man of God. When I was on earth a vision was revealed to me concerning the Edomites (the descendants of Esau). They were proud and for that the Lord showed me a vision of their downfall.

"The burden of the word of the Lord to Israel by Malachi.

I have loved you, saith the Lord. Yet ye say, Wherein hast thou loved us? Was not Esau Jacob's brother? saith the Lord: yet I loved Jacob,

And I hated Esau, and laid his mountains and his heritage waste for the dragons of the wilderness. Whereas Edom saith, We are impoverished, but we will return and build the desolate places; thus saith the Lord of hosts, They shall build, but I will throw down; and they shall call them, The border of wickedness, and, The people against whom the Lord hath indignation for ever." Malachi 1:1-4. Brother Paul, God hates pride, remember it was pride that caused Lucifer to loose his position before God.

"How art thou fallen from heaven, O Lucifer, son of the morning! how art thou cut down to the ground, which didst weaken the nations! For thou hast said in thine heart, I will ascend into heaven, I will exalt my throne above the stars of God: I will sit also upon the mount of the congregation, in the sides of the north: I will ascend above the heights of the clouds; I will be like the most High. Yet thou shalt be brought down to hell, to the sides of the pit." Isaiah 14: 12-15.

God resist the proud, but gives grace to the humble. The spirit of Pride is not of God but of the devil. It was pride that destroyed Lucifer in heaven when he thought to be as his creator. Hence, tell believers that have one spiritual gift or the other to remain humble and serve the Lord. Whether He gives you the ability to send rain on the earth, you must remain humble, for God resist the proud yet the humility is not of man's efforts but God imparts the grace for humility.

Elder 21: I was a prophet in my generation. I was bald headed. At a certain time in a certain land, their wickedness was much that it came to the presence of God. I was commanded to go and warn the inhabitants of the land that their wickedness has come before God. Instead of obeying God's instruction, I fled from His presence to another land.

"Now the word of the Lord came unto Jonah the son of Amittai, saying, Arise, go to Nineveh, that great city, and cry against it; for their wickedness is come up before Me. But Jonah rose up to flee unto Tarshish from the presence of the Lord, and went down to Joppa; and he found a ship going to Tarshish: so he paid the fare thereof, and went down into it, to go with them unto Tarshish from the presence of the Lord. But the Lord sent out a great wind into the sea, and there was a mighty tempest in the sea, so that the ship was like to be broken." Jonah 1:1-4.

Brother Paul, can a man run away from the creator of heaven and earth? Yet I attempted doing it and it almost cost me my life. There are men and women on earth that are supposed to be; great Prophet, Apostles, Evangelist, Teachers, Pastors and mighty vessels in God's hand but because of carelessness they rejected the calling of God for their lives. For this cause, God sends His wind against them as He did to the ship I boarded.

These ones are mostly faced with unending challenges because they abandoned the great commission of the most-high God. They live as a commoner instead of a king on earth. They are like the prodigal son who was supposed to be eating sumptuous meal in his father's house but because of the things of the world went into the world and met a great storm (hardship) and began to eat swine's food (from hand to mouth). These ones are sometimes given the grace because of the mercy of God, and at a point in their lives they may meet a servant of God who will tell them they have calling but are running away from the work of the GOD. Therefore, if they really want to make it in life they should go back to their calling and God will accept and re-ordain them in order to continue with His work on earth.

"Whither shall I go from Thy Spirit? or whither shall I flee from Thy presence? If I ascend up into heaven, Thou art there: if I make my bed in hell, behold, Thou art there. If I take the wings of the morning, and dwell in the uttermost parts of the sea; Even there shall Thy hand lead me, and Thy right hand shall hold me. If I say, Surely the darkness shall cover me; even the night shall be light about me. Yea, the darkness hideth not from Thee; but the night shineth as the day: the darkness and the light are both alike to Thee. For Thou hast possessed my reins: Thou hast covered me in my mother's womb."

Psalms 139:7-13

Elder 22: I am a prophet in Israel in the days of Jotham, Ahaz and Hezekiah, kings of Judah. I was told by God Almighty on the judgment that was going to come upon Israel and Judah. The Almighty God told the house of Jacob that their transgression was Samaria, and as for Judah their transgression was Jerusalem.

"The word of the Lord that came to Micah the Morasthite in the days of Jotham, Ahaz, and Hezekiah, kings of Judah, which he saw concerning Samaria and Jerusalem." Micah 1:1.

Brother Paul, the friends you go out with matters much. The scripture says;

"Iron sharpeneth iron; so a man sharpeneth the countenance of his friend." Proverbs 27:17.

The children of Israel were polluted and corrupted by the Samaritans, and the Lord told me to ask them "what have I done unto thee, and wherein have I wearied thee testify against me?

"O my people, what have I done unto thee? and wherein have I wearied thee? testify against me. For I brought thee up out of the land of Egypt, and redeemed thee out of the house of servants; and I sent before thee Moses, Aaron, and Miriam." Micah 6:3-4.

Brother Paul, our God is merciful even though the children of Judah were offering burnt offerings unto other gods on the high places in Jerusalem, gods that cannot see nor hear.

"Their idols are silver and gold, the work of men's hands. They have mouths, but they speak not: eyes have they, but they see not: They have ears, but they hear not: noses have they, but they smell not: They have hands, but they handle not: feet have they, but they walk not: neither speak they through their throat. They that make them are like unto them; so is every one that trusteth in them." Psalms 115:4-8.

But for the mercies of God on humanity, the messiah of the world came forth from Bethlehem of Judah, which is the smallest of the thousands of Judah. If God wants to lift a man up, He does it according to His divine will. Can you see how the savior of the World came out from the least clan in Judah?

Angel 14: The remaining two elders are talking with a saint that just arrived into the kingdom of our dear God. For now, let me take you to the hosts of the armies of our awesome GOD.

Chapter Sixteen: The Host of God

"Bless ye the Lord, all ye His hosts; ye ministers of his, that do His pleasure." Psalms 103:21

Host 1: Brother Paul, this group of Angels are called the seraphs, their task is to stand before God and play on the heavenly (musical) instruments, as they play, they abate the wrath of God upon humanity on earth because He is seated on His throne and sees how man is being wedded to a fellow man (sodomy), how a man changes his genital to that of a woman and woman to that of a man(transgender), how men through the pornographic films they watch, leave the normal gate that lead into the gift of marriage and enters through the window, in order to satisfy their flesh(abomination!). JEHOVAH sees all these things and laughs at the children of men. When the almighty God laughs it means that His wrath is about to be kindled.

"He that sitteth in the heavens shall laugh: the Lord shall have them in derision." Psalms 2:4.

So, this group of angels known as the Seraphs play before Him (Jehovah) to abate his anger:

"In the year that king Uzziah died I saw also the Lord sitting upon a throne, high and lifted up, and his train filled the temple. Above it stood the seraphims: each one had six wings; with twain he covered his face, and with twain he covered his feet, and with twain he did fly. And one cried unto another, and said, Holy, holy, holy, is the Lord of hosts: the whole earth is full of his glory. And the posts of the door moved at the voice of

him that cried, and the house was filled with smoke." Isaiah 6:1-4.

Host 2: Brother Paul, Are you aware that there are angels that are sent for ministration on earth? Have you not wondered that when a crusade is being held, millions and millions of souls will turn out in order to receive the blessings of God? This group of angels are in charge of ministration. They go there for the purpose of bringing souls unto repentance before the throne of God. The Holy Ghost convicts them (sinners) of their sins then these angels minister to them (sinners) to go out and accept the salvation of Jesus Christ after the conviction of their sins by the Holy Ghost.

"Are they not all ministering spirits, sent forth to minister for them who shall be heirs of salvation?" Hebrews 1:14.

Host 3: Brother Paul, when a man dies either by plane crash or motor accident, people of the world lament over the person's death; some would even challenge God saying "why will a holy man like this die this kind of death seeing that he pays his tithe, he goes from house for visitation, he gives alms to the poor, he goes for evangelism from one locality to the other, yet God allowed this man to die like this?" Some in their foolishness allows the devil to capture them through these incidents because the devil will begin to speak to them that "if a Holy man like that would die in an accident, how much less them that are still growing in faith?"

Through this, such a person could backslide. They are not wise before God and before the devil because they know that there is divine will of the Father. If it is the divine will of the Father, Nothing, I mean nothing can stop it in heaven, on earth and under the earth. If it is the divine will of the Father, even if three million great prophets come together and begin to pray for that situation to change, it can never change.

"But our God is in the heavens: He hath done whatsoever he hath pleased." Psalms 115:3.

Likewise in the Holy Scripture which believers are reading, day and night. We have holy men and women who were martyred for their faith. Some were burnt alive, some were crucified upside down, and some were beheaded. Yet these men were holy; holy before GOD.

"The righteous perisheth, and no man layeth it to heart: and merciful men are taken away, none considering that the righteous is taken away from the evil to come. He shall enter into peace: they shall rest in their beds, each one walking in his uprightness."Isaiah57:1-2.

So, is God wicked by allowing them to go through such painful death? It is His divine will and nothing can change it not even His Son Jesus Christ. Do you remember when the Son of man was about to be crucified, in the garden of Gethsemane He prayed to his Father telling him to take away the cup(suffering) from Him , nevertheless , not as He(Jesus) wills but as God (The Father) wills.

"Then cometh Jesus with them unto a place called Gethsemane, and saith unto the disciples, Sit ye here, while I go and pray yonder. And he went a little further, and fell on his face, and prayed, saying, O my Father, if it be possible, let this cup pass from me: nevertheless not as I will, but as thou wilt."Matthew 26:36, 39.

If the Son of God was not spared by the divine will of the Father, will man escape? Hence this group of angels are called the rescue angels if it is the will of God that a believer be rescued from any misfortune. He sends His angels who are for rescue even before the incident happens.

"For He shall give his angels charge over thee, to keep thee in all thy ways. They shall bear thee up in their hands, lest thou dash thy foot against a stone." Psalms 91:11-12.

Just as it happened in the holy scripture when Jonah was thrown into the sea in order to make the tempestuous sea against them cease, God in His infinite mercy had to send one of these rescue angels in the belly of the fish in order to preserve Jonah from dyeing. Likewise Paul the Apostle, when he was in the ship and there arose a tempestuous wind and the ship was caught and could not bear up into the wind, and the ship drove on her own.

Host 4: Brother Paul, this group of angels is before God saying holy, holy is the Lord God most high.

"And one cried unto another, and said, Holy, holy, holy, is the Lord of hosts: the whole earth is full of his glory." Isaiah6:2-3.

Host 5: This group of angels; are the angels of death, they are sent when Jehovah wants to wipe out the rebellious ones.

"And it came to pass, that at midnight the Lord smote all the firstborn in the land of Egypt, from the firstborn of Pharaoh that sat on his throne unto the firstborn of the captive that was in the dungeon; and all the firstborn of cattle. And Pharaoh rose up in the night, he, and all his servants, and all the Egyptians; and there was a great cry in Egypt; for there was not a house where there was not one dead." Exodus 12:29-30

"And when the angel stretched out his hand upon Jerusalem to destroy it, the Lord repented him of the evil, and said to the angel that destroyed the people, It is enough: stay now thine hand. And the angel of the Lord was by the threshing place of Araunah the Jebusite.

And David spake unto the Lord when he saw the angel that smote the people, and said, Lo, I have sinned, and I have done wickedly: but these sheep, what have they done? let thine hand, I pray thee, be against me, and against my father's house." 2 Samuel 24: 16-17.

"And the Lord sent an angel, which cut off all the mighty men of valour, and the leaders and captains in the camp of the

king of Assyria. So he returned with shame of face to his own land. And when he was come into the house of his god, they that came forth of his own bowels slew him there with the sword." 2 Chronicles 32:21.

Host 6: Brother Paul, this group of Angels; is in charge of the book of life. If believers on earth know what these angels do before God in HIS kingdom, they will not play with their firmness in God on earth. Do you know what these angels do before God? They erase the names of backsliders from the book of life and replace it with new converts.

"And the Lord said unto Moses, Whosoever hath sinned against Me, him will I blot out of My book." Exodus 32:33.

Host 7: Brother Paul this group of angels; welcomes saints immediately he or she arrives in heaven.

Host 8: Brother Paul, this group of angels; is called the guardian angels. God assigns them to whomever he wishes. There are men under the surface of the sun that God Almighty has assigned His angels to be going with them twenty four hours of the day and three hundred and sixty five days of the year. Any time they wake up in the morning, Satan trembles because he knows through these few (beloved saints) millions and millions of souls shall give their lives to Jesus in complete holiness.

"The angel of the Lord encampeth round about them that fear Him, and delivereth them."Psalms 34:7.

Host 9: This group of angels is assigned to be taking of records of those coming to church at the appointed time. They go to the various body of Christ (church-denominations) at just a minute to the stipulated time and are there with their spiritual book and pen. They record names of those coming to church on time. In a situation whereby a believer was in the Church to clean the sanctuary in preparation for the church worship service, and returns home to dress up for the church program, hence return late for the church service. Such a believer would not be recorded absent for his lateness but rather the time he came to clean the house of God will be recorded for him. However, those who came late as a result of carelessness will be recorded absent for that day.

Host 10: Brother Paul, haven't you wondered why men and women that are supposed to be listening to sermon in order to build their faith in God sleep while the sermon is going on? The reasons are either the hearers of the word are sinners or the preacher is a hypocrite. If the sinner from his or her heart wishes to listen to the sermon, the angels in charge will release grace for them to be awake and also fight demons so that the faithful ones (believers) does not sleep in the church. But most times sinners are often defeated because of their filthiness. On the other hand, if the preacher is a hypocrite, it becomes easy for demons to release their demonic fumes into the church, and immediately that is done members of the church will begin to dose within the space of five minutes.

Host 11: Brother Paul, this group of angels is the happiest whenever a sinner gives his life to God on earth.

"Likewise, I say unto you, there is joy in the presence of the angels of God over one sinner that repenteth." Luke15:10.

They are also the saddest when a believer backslides. Do you know why these angels are the happiest when a sinner gives his or her life to Jesus? It is because these angels are in charge of decorating the garments of believers in the kingdom of our dear God. Therefore when a sinner repents, a new garment is released from the throne of God for angelic decoration. Brother Paul, you can see that the way man think is not the way God thinks.

"For My thoughts are not your thoughts, neither are your ways My ways, saith the Lord." Isaiah5:5.

If it were to be man he will be angry that another garment is being brought for him to start decorating but praise God for He is not man and can never be a man. If a believer backslides back to sin, his garment is removed and kept aside should in case he repents and return to God.

"What man of you, having an hundred sheep, if he lose one of them, doth not leave the ninety and nine in the wilderness, and go after that which is lost, until he find it? And when he hath found it, he layeth it on his shoulders, rejoicing." Luke 15:4-5

Chapter Seventeen: Conversation With the Patriarchs of Old

(Nahum)

"The burden of Nineveh. The book of the vision of Nahum the Elkoshite." Nahum 1:1

Elder 23: Brother Paul, I am one of the strongest elder before God yet the youngest. The sins of Nineveh were revealed to me but their redemption was through elder 21. That land was highly sinful before God just like the land of Sodom and Gomorrah. However, they humbled themselves before God when they were warned to depart from their sins by elder 21.

If sinners on earth will humble themselves before God and come with a repentant heart, our dear god will have mercy on them and forgive their sins. *"He that covereth his sins shall not prosper: but whoso confesseth and forsaketh them shall have mercy."Proverbs 28:13.*

"If we confess our sins, He is faithful and just to forgive us our sins, and to cleanse us from all unrighteousness."1John1:9.

Angel 15: Brother Paul, when you go back to the world, tell them that the Son of man is about to come and take his bride home. Let all men come to God so that they will have everlasting life. The last elder wants to take you round the kingdom of God and show you **"The jumpers at the gate of hell"**.

Chapter Eighteen: The Son of God

The Last Elder: Paul, everyone; angels, holy beast, saints and elders have told you the mysteries of the kingdom of God and the deceit of the kingdom of darkness. Hence, you have been equipped to proclaim the goodness of our dear God to them that will make it when the rapture shall take place or when they sleep in the Lord.

Brother Paul, did you remember Him that met you along that tunnel of hell and told you "don't do don't do, I AM the one. *I AM the beginning and the end, the first and the last, the God that was, that is and is to come, GOD ALMIGHTY. I AM He that was dead and yet alive; I AM the bright and the morning star, the ancient of days, the beginning and the end. I hold the key of life and death. To them that shall allow Me come into their hearts, I shall be their GOD and they shall be My people and I shall give them the power to eat from the tree of life. I shall give them a white stone that has a name which no one knows except him that receives the stone from My hand. Before Abraham was I AM, before the first elder I AM, I was redeemed from the dead by the power of My Father and I sit at the right hand of My Father. I am the first and the last elder before My Farther, I AM GOD"*.

"I am Alpha and Omega, the beginning and the ending, saith the Lord, which is, and which was, and which is to come, the Almighty.

I am Alpha and Omega, the first and the last: and, What thou seest, write in a book, and send it unto the seven churches which are in Asia; unto Ephesus, and unto Smyrna, and unto

Pergamos, and unto Thyatira, and unto Sardis, and unto Philadelphia, and unto Laodicea.

I am he that liveth, and was dead; and, behold, I am alive for evermore, Amen; and have the keys of hell and of death."
Revelation 1:8, 11 and 18.

My glory will I not share with any man and my glory will I not give to dogs (sinners). I have given humanity life and life upon life to them that shall let Me into their heart, I will transform them and make them victorious over Satan, death and sin. But to them that shall not allow Me, I will make them dine with the devil in the pit of hell forever.

__Jumpers At the Gate of Hell__ are men and women who their abomination is too great before God that there is no space to write their evil deeds, therefore, their book of judgment are sent into the kingdom of darkness for the devil to judge them. They are not given the privilege to see the throne of judgment. They are so abominable before the Father, the Son and the Holy Ghost. When they die, they are immediately carried by the stormy wind of God into the region of darkness. When these JUMPERS at the GATE of HELL were alive, because of their filthiness, their souls travel towards the tunnel of hell, instead of the broad road. Hence if they die, they will not be given the privilege to plead for their sins before the throne of GOD.

Paul you were a __Jumper at the Gate of Hell__ but because of the divine agreement from the throne of My Father, We decided to rescue you by sending a holy beast into that spiritual tunnel of hell. Men on earth are so foolish that they will change their genital organs and still want Me (the everlasting God) to judge them. Tell them that I say there is no judgment for them but everlasting torment. Men on earth are so foolish that they will sell their souls to the devil by joining "dreaded" secret cult. Tell them that immediately they die without repentance, their father the devil will judge them. Men on earth are so foolish that they engage in same sex marriage (Sodomy); tell them that if they die without repenting their father the devil will conduct the main spiritual wedding for both of them in the pit of hell. There is no judgment for these ones because they are so abominable before my Father, I and the Holy Ghost.

"He that hath an ear, let him hear what the Spirit saith unto the churches; To him that overcometh will I give to eat of the tree of life, which is in the midst of the paradise of God." Revelation 2:7.